From Vulnerable to Invincible

Achieve, succeed and live a more fulfilling life

Sarah Jones

Sarah-J Coaching

United Kingdom

For more information, see https://sarah-j.com/

Book Layout © 2018 MyAuthorlyFormatting.com

ISBN 978-1-9996672-0-7

FOREWORD

How I am qualified to write this book? Well, everything is based on my own experiences, and I know I'm not the only one to have been through these challenges or similar, and these are transferable skills. I have an innate drive to 'be my best self.' I am aware this came from childhood, when my father was very ill for some time, and it taught me very quickly that life is for living, and we must make the best of this experience. It was a difficult time for our family, and I'm sure many families, and perhaps you, have been through terribly challenging situations. I am grateful though that it gave me my energy and spirit to enjoy my life and overcome other challenges thrown at me.

I've had over twenty years of experience in the commercial environment—in organisations of all sizes and going through all sorts of corporate changes. Mergers, acquisitions, takeovers, outsourcing, restructuring—you name it! I've led teams of all sizes, both in the UK and overseas. I've run my own freelance PR business for several years... and I re-qualified as a business, career, executive and personal coach over four years ago. I've coached on subjects ranging from confidence, leadership, conflict, setting up new businesses, career changes, complete life overhauls, and time management, through to stress and overwhelm... and have successfully helped clients to recalibrate and disrupt negative and limiting behaviours.

So, you may be at a crossroads in your career, business, personal life or both—well don't worry—I'll provide you with insights and exercises to help you move from feeling a little shaky and a little vulnerable, to feeling invincible and on top of the world!

Very often self-development may feel very serious, or boring. But it can certainly be enjoyable... it's fun to get to know yourself and understand what's important. With this book and a little time and energy, you're now in a position to have the tools to do this. Enjoy the process!

CONTENTS

INTRODUCTION

Have you ever had the feeling that something just doesn't feel right? That you don't feel you are on the right path? That you are dancing to the beat of someone else's drum?

This book covers three key stages that may just help you answer these questions. I'll show you how you can start to embrace your vulnerability, and your fears, and use them to galvanise you forward.

To do this, you must face some of your fears. This creates the space for you to truly consider who you are: your genuine, authentic self. Often when we act on our fears—and do not recognise or accept who we are—it creates all kinds of stress in both our personal and professional lives. Being authentic, in my mind, is the key to happiness.

And once you have tackled those areas? Well, the sky's the limit! Yes, there are often setbacks in life, but if you are genuinely on the right path, and understand yourself, you're very much headed towards invincibility.

When you read those questions above, you may either be screaming 'yes that's me' or even 'well actually on paper everything is good but I'm just not happy or fulfilled.'

I've experienced both of those feelings above in my life, personally and professionally. I've often compared this feeling to having a vaguely rumbling stomach, which over time builds into immense hunger pains that won't go away until you've fed them!

And boy did I feed them with all kinds of distractions. Nights out, holidays, clothes… yes, it was all great fun as I'm a 'glass half-full person,' but they did not resolve the niggling feeling in my gut that I was just not being true to myself!

I had a classic photocopier moment, that moment of clarity and insight, after watching Wayne Dyer's 'The Shift'—which I recommend—where I realised, 'I can't do what I am doing anymore.' And I made my own shift. I travelled round Mexico for three months, cave diving, and driving around. Having that space was necessary. (By the way, I highly recommend road trips for a change of scene, thinking space and all that!)

Whilst abroad, I realised the meaning of 'life is a journey,' and whilst it sounds cliched, it's true. We are all shaped by experiences as we travel through life (e.g. redundancy, divorce, illness, financial difficulties, conflict). If we notice our own reactions and behaviours are not serving us well, we may take active steps to modify behaviours through self-development, coaching or therapy, and peel away certain layers of our own onion, as it were. And age and experience may also shape us along the way.

And let's face it—life is never done. We don't finish it. Life is a collection of moment-by-moment experiences and decisions we make, and their cause and effect. If you are someone who wants to evolve and make the most of your life experience, you will understand that we are all on our own paths—even though sometimes they don't make sense—but we are never the finished the article. Yes, you may be someone who is happy in their comfort zone and that's fine, but you'll never know which experiences will shape you or how! But the chances are if you are reading this, the following thoughts may have crossed your mind:

- I want more, but I don't know what more is!
- I know this doesn't feel right, but I can't see the wood for the trees
- I'm really unhappy—I'm going through the motions or on a constant treadmill
- I feel like I am putting on a mask, I am not myself—I'm acting
- I can't be myself—what will people think?
- It's too late, I'm too young, I'm too old, it's too difficult… so I'll stay where I am
- Everyone else seems happy, why aren't I?

- I've got no good reason to be unhappy, I'm being self-indulgent and selfish
- It's not that bad really
- I've worked so hard to get here, it's going to be so difficult to change

The problem is we can only ignore these feelings for so long. After a while they can result in the following:

- Unhealthy behaviours and distractions
- Unhealthy relationships
- Coming up against the same situations again and again with poor results
- Rising stress levels
- Taking frustrations out on other people and reacting badly
- Career dissatisfaction and lack of progress
- No clear purpose, vision and plan in your life
- No clear idea of who you are or what makes you tick... what makes you *you*
- Lack of motivation and procrastination
- A bad dose of the 'shoulda, woulda, coulda'

If you recognise any of yourself in this introduction, this book is definitely for you and it will teach you to go from:

Vulnerable to Authentic to Invincible

HOW TO GO FROM VULNERABLE TO INVINCIBLE

When I thought about the title, *From Vulnerable to Invincible,* I realised there was a missing step: authenticity. This may be an area you have considered before, or not, but in my experience, and that of many of my clients, there tends to be an underlying discomfort or unhappiness when we know we are not being true to ourselves. Perhaps we are bending to the whims of others. Perhaps we just don't know who we are and what we want... Being authentic is therefore an important step to include.

I know I am not very good at pretending, and I see that as raw honesty. Perhaps you feel the same, or that you are living your life according to someone else's agenda, or compromising what you really, truly want in life. As I mentioned, your agenda can change depending on what has happened, and has yet to happen in your life, and how you move through life events and phases.

These are big concepts to work with, so I'm going to use what's known as a three by three approach to break down the key themes—of vulnerability, authenticity and invincibility—into manageable steps. I don't know about you but breaking down concepts works for me. Having some kind of structure to the great big picture that is life allows me to identify what's going on, make changes, and review my progress. Otherwise, tackling the whole, big picture is overwhelming. It's too big to handle, and it makes it far too easy to find distractions or procrastinate.

So that's where my stepwise approach has come from—it's a method or way to help you break the exercises and themes down into manageable pieces, and for you to identify where you are, and monitor progress.

With each situation, we may find ourselves veering between the scales. For example, we may have a total grip on our professional lives, but we start a new relationship that presents its own situations and challenges. We need to recalibrate, adjust and figure out how to bring two lives, or aspects of our lives, together, and sometimes that presents situations where we may feel vulnerable or uncomfortable. It may even give rise to limiting beliefs about ourselves, or sabotaging behaviours that prevent us reaching our full potential.

So, let's get going. Let's start with vulnerability.

VULNERABILITY

YOUR GREATEST STRENGTH IF YOU LET IT IN

Vulnerable: Exposed to the possibility of being attacked or harmed, either physically or emotionally.[1]

Vulnerability: Open to moral attack, criticism, temptation, etc.[2]

It's tough, this vulnerability stuff. It's very often the time in life when we want to run away the most. Personally, I've actually experienced the sensation of burning, itching feet in the past. Luckily, I found that by sitting with the very feeling of not being comfortable, I managed to work through these difficult emotions and physical feelings.

When you tackle vulnerability, like any skill, it becomes easier to do over time. Yes, you may have to go through some discomfort, but when we move out

---

[1] https://en.oxforddictionaries.com/definition/vulnerable
[2] http://www.dictionary.com/browse/vulnerability

of our comfort zones into stretch zones, this is where the real progress is made. And if we do it step-by-step, we won't fall into feeling that we're totally overwhelmed.

And the bad news—well, it's good if you think about it—we don't get to choose when we feel vulnerable. We have to allow those situations, or people in, that can make us feel vulnerable.

It's your truth, and it's part of who you are, linking you to your authentic self.

What does vulnerability feel like? How do I know if I'm feeling vulnerable?

Here are some insights based on my own experiences, and those of my clients:

- Feeling afraid that if I ask for what I want it will turn out wrong
- Feeling afraid to speak out
- Feeling in danger or under threat, or attacked
- Feeling I have no choice but to accept this situation
- Wanting to flee, or run away, from an unpleasant situation
- Avoiding people, situations or discussions
- Overtly arguing or acting defensively
- Resorting to behaviours that are very parental (e.g. scolding, reprimanding, critical) with others

- Resorting to childish type behaviours (outbursts, name calling) with others
- Feeling you can't trust others to see you or accept you when you are vulnerable

Vulnerability can feel raw. You may feel weak or exposed, but that's alright. It helps us get to the real roots of who we are.

And actually, as much as you push against it, you won't always have a choice about whether you feel vulnerable or not. If you want to live a full life, and achieve your dreams and goals, you will feel vulnerable, and exposed, at some point.

However, take the opportunity to reframe vulnerability, and see it as a strength, and your greatest opportunity for progress.

WHEN IT'S NOT SO GOOD

As weird as this may sound to you, our most uncomfortable situations or relationships with people can be our greatest teachers.

Have you ever had a situation where it felt terrible, or hopeless at the time, and yet it turned out really well? If you can recall these situations, you can reflect on them to comfort yourself in any vulnerable position you may find yourself in in the future.

Here are some situations I've been in to give you a guide, and I'm sure you can think of situations you've been in, where you've felt just as exposed:

- Being front and centre of major corporate events where I'm leading the corporate communications function, and not having all the answers to-hand
- Being asked to lead teams who are not functioning, during times of major change, where the team is not open to that change and is openly hostile to me
- Dealing with major risks and crises in a business with little or no notice
- Having to push back to people in organisations more senior to myself and who were very overbearing
- Pushing back to key clients on flawed messages and strategies when working in PR agencies
- Being in a personal relationship and listening to someone's feedback and reaction to my behaviour that was totally 'out of the blue'
- Entering a relationship when there are make or break issues to iron out, and letting go of the consequence of speaking up
- Being newly promoted into a role but not really knowing much about leadership
- Telling someone how I feel about them for the first time

- And meeting their friends, family, and even children from a former relationship
- Being with a partner where the previous partner still plays a part due to children
- Facing redundancy, or a major restructure or change to my role, team or organisation
- Facing illness or injury
- Major financial issues or difficulties
- Speaking a conference or event
- Meeting new people in work or social situations
- Moving to a new location, or even country
- Starting up a new business or changing an existing one

I can't cover every situation, but I'm sure you can write your own list.

Exercise: reflect back and ask yourself the following questions:

- When did I feel vulnerable?
- What did I do about it?
- How did that work out?
- What could I have done differently?
- What are the signs that I feel vulnerable?

This will help you watch out for those times when you feel really raw and uncomfortable. and maybe want to run and avoid a situation? Or maybe you feel you need to control the situation, impose your will, control, act defensively and dictate to others because you cannot allow yourself to feel vulnerable? These are all signs to watch out for.

Now we've covered the signs and situations where you may feel uncomfortable, here are just a couple of exercises to help you to work through this.

Exercise: Just sit still

Whenever you feel raw and uncomfortable, just stop. Find somewhere quiet and sit. Don't run away or deflect your feelings onto others. Accept yourself and acknowledge how you are feeling. Sit there for as long as it takes, not to suppress any thoughts or emotions, but to truly allow them in, until you can sit comfortably with them or they subside. This avoids negatively feeding that vulnerable feeling, letting it run away with you, and allowing it to become a lifestyle choice. Just accept it.

Exercise: Ask yourself questions

Grab a notebook and write down the answers to the following questions. Review your answers a little later on, or the next day. This gives you the space and time to master your situation instead of reacting to it:

• How am I feeling?

- Where have I had this feeling before?
- What is it telling me?
- What do I truly want in this situation?
- What do I want to communicate?
- What other steps do I take?
- How will I deal with difficult feelings if they arise again?
- What can I change, to influence this situation for the good?
- Repeat—what do I truly want from this situation?
- What good may come from this situation?

Getting things down on paper stops them swirling around in our minds. Looking at something on paper enables us to review things more objectively and takes the sting out of them.

Exercise: Direct your energy elsewhere

This is not avoidance, but something to take the distract yourself from the negative emotions that have surfaced. For example, here are some things I've done that have allowed me to process my strong feelings:

- Connect with a friend and go out
- Meditate
- Writing down my feelings
- Saying positive statements to myself
- Just sitting with it allowing those feelings to pass

- Exercising to increases endorphins and feel good hormones
- Watching a movie
- Taking a bath
- Watching a comedy sketch
- Smiling to increase the dopamine flow in our body
- Talk to a supportive, objective party, whether friend or colleague

Things that don't work include moaning, criticising, walling off, being defensive, lack of sleep, poor eating or drinking too much. These just feeds those negative feelings. They are short-term fixes which keep you in a place that does not allow for positive growth, development or happiness.

WHEN IT'S GOOD

Dr Brené Brown, an expert on vulnerability, says:

"Vulnerability is the core of shame, fear and a struggle for worthiness, but it appears that it is also the birthplace of joy, of creativity, belonging, and love."

You can get to a place where these uncomfortable feelings can catapult you to greater strength if you face them head on. Yes, you may still need time to process what is happening to you but tackling those vulnerability issues will make you stronger as a leader, as a partner. I guarantee it. It's like going to the gym;

we work out and develop certain muscle groups, improve strength and stamina. We need to do that with our minds as well! It doesn't just happen unless we make it a conscious practice!

Try the exercises I outlined above a few times and you will start to recognise when you are feeling vulnerable and in danger of engaging with unhealthy and damaging behaviours. When you recognise something, you can deal with it. Here are some 'before and afters' that I've experienced myself, and transformations that my clients have been through:

Example 1

- **Before: ignoring vulnerability**
  - *I'll blame others and criticise them, or*
  - *I'll just keep myself to myself and wall off*
- **After: accepting vulnerability**
  - *I will review my own behaviour and think about how to address my concerns*
- **Results of accepting vulnerability**
  - *I realise I have misconstrued the situation*
  - *I realise that others have a different view that is valid*
  - *I realise there are some reactions and behaviours I need to change*
  - *I realise I have contributed to this situation*

- *Misconceptions are cleared up leading to greater harmony, happiness and positive relationships*

Example 2

- **Before: ignoring vulnerability**
  - *I'll just quit my job or put up with it*
- **After: accepting vulnerability**
  - *I will review where I am in my career, and openly address matters with my manager and/or team*
- **Results of accepting vulnerability**
  - *Awareness there has been a misunderstanding*
  - *Career development prospects open up*
  - *Leading a project to cultivate the change you have highlighted*
  - *Enhanced relationships at work*
  - *Additional training, mentoring or coaching is provided*
  - *Additional resource provided*
  - *Reconfiguration of policies*
  - *Opportunities for the team open up*
  - *Sharing of frustrations to allow for team building and development*

Example 3

- **Before: ignoring vulnerability**
  - *I won't say how I feel*

- **After: accepting vulnerability**
    - *I will say how I feel in a calm, adult manner*
- **Results of accepting vulnerability**
    - *Strengthened relationships with others based on respect, trust and mutual understanding. Learning that others do not see things the way you do but compromise and agreement can be reached*

Example 4

- **Before: ignoring vulnerability**
    - *I'll just leave the relationship*
- **After: accepting vulnerability**
    - *I will speak to the other person about how I feel and what needs to change*
- **Results of accepting vulnerability**
    - *The relationship is improved, and we make agreements as a couple*
    - *Misconceptions and assumptions are cleared up*
    - *Greater harmony, happiness and intimacy*
    - *The relationship ends, and I am free to find someone else that can meet my needs—I have done the best I can, which I cannot regret*

Checking In!

Does any of this sound familiar? Have you had situations that you have misinterpreted? How did it feel to use the 'before' behaviour? What about the 'after' behaviour? Where can you start to make some changes?

STEPPING INTO VULNERABILITY

Exercise: internal dialogue, external reactions

Here are some questions, which you can use if you are avoiding, or reacting to key situations:

- What am I saying to myself, about myself when this happens, when I feel most exposed?
- How does that think affect my reactions?
- And how do I tend to react?
- What is the result of that reaction?
- What do I would I like to happen?
- What would I rather say to myself?

Look at your answers. Now really dig deep and think about what you are telling yourself. Your inner voice reflects itself in your body language, spoken language and behaviours. It works from the inside out—cause and effect—to create a reaction, and often that leads into shutdown mode and the feeling:

'See I knew this would happen'

This is a very convenient reaction because it means we can blame everyone and everything outside of ourselves, rather than take responsibility for our actions and their consequences in our lives.

If you do this, you're not the only one. Don't beat yourself up about it! And with each step forward and new situations, you may feel 'less than' and vulnerable. Please don't be harsh on yourself—be your own best friend-recognise that you are not serving your best interests, and that you are in defensive mode, to protect yourself. Rather than letting it hold yourself back, notice it and ask the following questions:

- How can I improve this situation, or make it work for me?
- What do I need to say to myself to make that happen?

Then ask:

- What negative things do I say to myself e.g. I'm not worthy, it will never work, just forget it, I'll never do it, I don't know what to do?
- What phrases run through my mind?
- What positive phrases, or beliefs, could I replace them with?

These positive phrases are called affirmations. And there is plenty of evidence to show we can re-wire our brains to think more positively, rather like rebooting the hard drive of a computer. It takes time and effort but if you do it often enough, like anything, it will become easier and an established habit., A default pattern, where you start to recognise negative phrases, and think "hang on, what else could I say instead?" is one of the best ways to deal with feeling vulnerable.

These affirmations should be short statements, using positive words, denoting forwards movement. They should also use words that mean something to you, and that you can resonate with. For example:

- I am becoming more comfortable in all situations
- I face situations head-on
- I can choose my reactions
- I listen to the views of others
- I am open to change
- I am okay letting go of the need to control
- I am amazing!

Each different situation may require a new phrase. Write them down to enforce them—write them at least ten times every day in your journal and say them to yourself regularly. Even better, try standing in front of the mirror, looking yourself in the eye and repeating them to yourself. It's uncomfortable, particularly to start with, but it's a gentle way of allowing yourself to be vulnerable.

Believing you can accept difficult or challenging situations will help you make the most of these great learning experiences. This is how I took the step to start up my own business, twice, when everyone said I was crazy! I did it anyway, despite coming from an upbringing, and in a time when it was not particularly considered wise to set up on your own, and in a recession. I learnt to choose to share my goals with supporters only!

So, let's recap:

We've discussed the concept of vulnerability to authenticity to invincibility.

We've discovered what vulnerability is, and how it shows up in different situations.

We've covered when vulnerability is bad, and the negative impact it can have on you.

And we've explored how to make the most of vulnerability and make it work for you.

By now, you should have your own notes from the exercises, as well as my personal examples to help you tackle vulnerability head on.

These are big subjects, but by now, you should be recognising situations that appear to be negative, see how they can be our greatest forms of progress, and know what you can do to adapt and learn from them.

Next stop: authenticity!

AUTHENTICITY

PUT DOWN THE MASK AND LAY THE FOUNDATIONS FOR THE REAL YOU

Authenticity means being true to yourself, being genuine, the real you, credible, believable, trustworthy... These are all words associated with authenticity. And this relates to vulnerability, because when you are at your most exposed, authenticity can be the core of who you are.

Very often we can go through life not being ourselves, or only in certain situations. Certainly, life is often about compromises (I prefer the word *choices*) but only you can know what is true for you, and how to be true to yourself. I firmly believe you can only dance to the beat of someone else's tune for so long before that nagging feeling builds up and results in a major change, for example walking out of a job, or a relationship. Sometimes we wait until things become unbearable, letting them build and build, until eventually, we pop like a cork.

However, if we are self-aware and know what's important to us, and what drives us, we have a good chance of making what I call 'course corrections' or 'degree shifts' along the way. It means we act from the front foot, we don't have to have some kind of catastrophic meltdown, filled with regret because we have over-compromised, but make shifts along the way instead.

If you do have a big 'showdown' or 'meltdown,' it's not the end of the world either. You've just realised something that you either were not quite aware of, or ready to face before, and something has tipped you over the edge that now you cannot run away from. There's a saying that many people change when the pain of staying the same, in the same place, outweighs any pain of change.

There's also a great saying from Thomas Merton:

"People can spend their whole lives climbing the ladder of success only to find, once they reach the top, that it's leaning across the wrong wall."

Basically, by not being yourself or true to what you want, you can waste a whole lot of time, and a whole lot of life. Not a great idea that, is it?

For me, being authentic actually means being honest, both with myself and other people. Not to the point of being rude, but I do believe in being clear with people, and to that end I am fairly comfortable in situations that others may find difficult. But I still have areas I've had to work on myself in, as I alluded to earlier. There's always been a guiding light of wanting to be the best version of me, for myself, and for others, and to live each day to its very best. Of course, we all have off days, and sometimes, we just have to ride them out.

My belief came as a result of having a very ill family member from a young age and seeing how important it is to value all of our experiences in life and turn adversities into strengths. So, for me, authenticity means being honest, true to my core, and is something that leads and encourages happiness, and the ability and freedom to make changes if needed.

However, what does authenticity mean to you? You may have your own ideas. Start to think about it and make some notes.

WHEN WE ARE NOT AUTHENTIC: HOW THINGS GO AWRY

You may have an idea of where you are not being yourself, or over-compromising, or pretending. Perhaps even feeling a bit numb in life or to what is happening around you. Here are some examples to help you:

- You are in a job but struggling and going through the motions

- You have considered a job change more than once over the last few months
- You are seriously unhappy in a relationship and roll your eyes at your partner
- You can't make the choices you want to in your career?
- When people describe you, you don't like what you hear, and it shocks you?
- You can't sleep
- You struggle to get up in the morning
- You are struggling in your position at work—as a leader, or employee
- You are struggling to get any ventures off the ground
- You want to make changes but are scared of what others will say and think
- You are unhappy more often than unhappy
- You don't think your needs are important
- You are putting on a mask at work, or at social events with family etc...
- You are trying to be authentic—i.e. it's not second nature

So, when you look at these examples, and how it can affect your health, happiness, relationships and success, how important do you think it is to be authentic?

I would suggest extremely. Accept that it's important. Accept that your need to be your real self is authentic. Realise that happiness, and fulfilment, comes from the inside out. You have to be in pole position to be happy in yourself and who you are, before you can make anyone else happy, or affect external circumstances.

It's not overnight work. And there are always tweaks. As I mentioned before, each change or adaption makes way for additional changes and adaptions—be open and welcome them in. Life isn't a full stop, but a series of semi-colons.

WHAT DOES AUTHENTICITY LOOK LIKE?

Have you ever met someone, or worked with someone who you just connected with, and who oozed personality, generosity and kindness, even when things got tough? You may have had moments like that yourself and recognised it yourself, when even difficult situations just seem manageable, because you are in the flow.

I remember working with a CEO and I just have the utmost respect for him even to this day. Why? Because he was passionate about customer service, which is one of my key values. It wasn't just one of those corporate values trotted out. He lived it and breathed it. It was consistent in his words and actions and what he expected of others… it was genuine. He also listened, would take advice, and valued other's opinions—all great values as a leader. I feel privileged to have worked alongside him. He made an impact on me as a role model, because of his authentic values and qualities.

Believe me when I tell you it's easier to be honest with yourself and others, and be authentic, than to put up a pretence. Pretending can be stressful and draining. There will be situations that are new, alien and out of your comfort zone, but authenticity means more than that. When you are not being authentic, you are not being yourself, and it impacts on what you do, how you do it, and who you are with.

If you are a motivated, go-getting individual who wants to make the best of your life—which I assume you are if you have read this far—I'm going to assume that those nagging, doubting thoughts are growing in volume.

Authenticity is a state of living, not an object you can own. So, it literally starts with you.

Exercise: what's your authenticity?

- Write down 'authenticity' on a piece of paper and think about what other words come to mind? What does it mean to you?
- Where and when are you authentic in your life?
- Where and when do you believe you may be over-compromising, or pretending not to be yourself?
- How does that feel?

- What does this lack of authenticity stop you doing?
- What would you be like as a person do if you could be truly authentic?

YOUR VALUES: WHAT MAKES YOU TICK?

This is a very brief snapshot of a big subject and may help introduce you to your own authenticity. Values are individual to each of us—they are our internal 'sat nav' that guides us. Typically, our core values stay with us for most of our lives, but they can adapt and evolve as we grow older. As we mature, things happen to us in life, and usually we need some form of this 'value' to be present, to feel fulfilled.

In this instance, 'values' in this instance is not a judgement word or about taking the moral high-ground. It's simply a word to describe something you need in your life to be fulfilled or feel on course. They are single words such as respect, achievement, love.

Let me give you a personal example: I've spent years doing deep, adventurous scuba diving. I wondered what draws me to it when other people recoil at the mere idea? Having looked at my values, to me it's about adventure and excitement. As I've grown older, I still want to go diving now and again—maybe on holiday, maybe some adventurous stuff—but it's not the priority it once was. By knowing myself, and what makes me tick—aligning my goals with my values-I know that I need to weigh up 'balance' with 'adventure.' It's an adjustment of how I spend my time, and still get some down time.

Exercise: Your Values

Look at the following words. They reflect common values that people tend to have or want in their lives. Circle your top ten and make your own list of key values that are important for you in your life.

Acceptance	Achievement
Adaptability	Adventure
Affection	Atheneite
Autonomy	Balance
Beauty	Assertiveness
Altruism	Caring
Cleanliness	Contribution
Compassion	Compassion
Creativity	Curiosity
Determination	Development
Different	Excitement
Fun	Faith
Family	Freedom
Friendship	Fun
Growth	Happiness
Individual	Integrity
Joy	Justice

Kindness	Leadership
Learning	Legacy
Love	Loyalty
Modesty	Neatness
Openness	Optimism
Order	Play
Power	Praise
Peace	Praise
Relationships	Relaxation
Religion	Reliable
Resilience	Responsibility
Respect	Rest
Results	Risk
Safety	Security
Self-respect	Serenity
Service	Significance
Solitude	Spirituality
Stability	Success
Support	Status
Teamwork	Tolerance
Trustworthy/trust	Wealth
Wisdom	

Keep your list and think about what's important to you. You can have more than ten but start here. Think about what matters to you in your personal, social and work life.

Additional exercise

Ask yourself:
- What this word means to you?
- How this value needs to show up in your life?
- Where does this value rank in your list 1–10

Remember this is about you, and you alone. Of course, you can share them with people who are important to you, but this is personal, no judging yourself here!

Authenticity is often listed as a value and I have included it here but as we've discussed, it's more than a value, it's about how we show up in our lives.

More questions to ask yourself

Top five qualities about you! What makes you… you?

What top five qualities are most important to you? What makes you unique? Write them down, and ask your friends and family, as sometimes other people can see what we cannot see ourselves.

What makes you feel alive?

Don't spend too long on this. Have a think about the following, and scribble away for ten to fifteen minutes. It's useful to reflect on what you've written in the days and months to come.

- What do you like to do that makes the time fly by?
- What made you really happy as a young child?
- What are your top five or ten joys and passions in life?
- What does this tell you about yourself?

When people annoy you: clues to yourself

Remember I mentioned that our toughest moment and toughest opponents can be our greatest teachers? Well, very often those difficult characters can reveal a lot about ourselves, especially if you find yourself jealous of someone.

Ask yourself, "what is it that I recognise or am likely repressing in myself that can see in the other person?"

I've had this in past with various bosses and realised it was actually a facet within myself that needed developing... my confidence!

Also, these people or situations can give us clues about our values. Which value of mine is being squashed or suppressed? Does this person represent the opposite of one of my personal values? For example, if you value freedom then you'll resent being controlled. Your reaction will give you massive clues into recognising there's something you need to develop in yourself, or that a value you hold is being repressed.

All this information makes you uniquely and authentically you, and understanding it helps you grow into yourself. And no two people are the same: how you perceive the value of a choice, or routine, may be very different to how friends, colleagues, partners or others perceive them.

HOW TO UNLEASH YOUR AUTHENTICITY

Now that we've covered what authenticity is—what it looks like, what can happen if you are not being authentic, what it means to you, and what makes you tick—here are few ideas to help you become more authentic, genuine and real, so you can truly live your life.

Your purpose or 'why'

Many of us consider big questions such as:

- What is driving me?
- What is my purpose in life?
- Why am I here?
- Why am I doing this?

If we know (or try and discover) the underlying reasons for why we do what we do, and what is important to us, it can tell us a lot about the activities we follow and the actions we choose.

And sometimes, when we feel a little off course, knowing our purpose helps get us back on the right track.

Introduction to purpose

While I firmly believe that 'being happy' is the overriding purpose in life, if we want to make a change in life, it is important to understand our purpose, our 'why'.

Understanding this will help you work out what motivates you, what is important to you, and what excites you. Chances are that you may not even be aware of what this is. Too many of us don't know. Being aware of your purpose will help you align your goals and aims in life and motivate you to achieve exactly what you want to achieve, even when the going gets tough.

Try not to struggle with this though, keep it simple if you need to. The aim is to find out what gives you a life filled with passion and meaning, and you can still do that without fully knowing your purpose. You may even have more than one theme. For example, mine is really simple: 'make the most of life, have fun, and help others along the way.' That can translate into a million different things! Some people have more detailed purposes, for example 'to live in great peace and awareness and create that for others.'

Finding your purpose

It's important to be completely relaxed for this exercise. Try not to force it but find a quiet place that makes you feel comfortable and where you're not going to be disturbed. Remember that everyone has a unique purpose, and sometimes this has been born out of our past experiences. Some people just know what this purpose is, others of us have to dig a little bit deeper, especially if it is not something you have considered before.

Have a think about *why* you want to know your purpose, ask "how will it help me?" With me, it helped me to ensure that my goals were aligned to my purpose and values, rather than doing things I thought I 'should' be doing.

Exercise: Finding Your Purpose

Get a piece of paper and write on it 'My Life's Purpose' and just write down what pops into your head! It doesn't have to be about saving the universe. It should be fun and exciting, and will give you a benchmark for what's important and makes you tick...

- What's important to me and how I spend my time?
- What do you like to do that makes the time fly by?
- What really moves you?

- What problem would you like to solve for the world?
- If you only had a week to solve a problem, or do what you wanted to do, what would it be?

This can help to lead you to who you are at your core and give more insight into what's important to you.

MINDFULNESS

Mindfulness is something you may find a useful tool as you strive to uncover who you really want to be, and what makes you tick. It links to authenticity because it allows you to take life moment-by-moment, bit-by-bit. Rather than immediately reacting, it gives you space and time to think. This is vital when tackling vulnerability and authenticity.

There's a lot that's been written on this subject, and it's a practice that's being introduced to organisations as it has gained recognition as something that helps people manage and cope with stress. People who practise mindfulness play a fuller part in their life, situations and relationships, and make more informed, better decisions. The UK Government's National Institute for Health and Clinical Excellence (NICE) recommends mindfulness. for the treatment of recurrent depression.

I've taken a summary of mindfulness from their website as it summarises it perfectly:

"Typically, mindfulness practice involves sitting with your feet planted on the floor and the spine upright. The eyes can be closed or rest a few feet in front while the hands are in the lap or on the knees. The attention is gently brought to rest on the sensations of the body—the feet on the floor, the pressure on the seat and the air passing through the nostrils. As the thoughts continue, you return again and again to these physical sensations, gently encouraging the mind not to get caught up in the thought processes but to observe their passage."[3]

Take the time to do this on a regular basis, whenever, or anywhere that you are comfortable to do so. I often use it and it works. It's a technique to use whenever you feel overwhelmed, as it gives you space for composure and thought. Sometimes, during those spaces, we find out more about ourselves because we have given ourselves pause to do so. It will certainly help you in situations where you feel vulnerable, but also help you to get in touch with your authentic self over time and as you start to gain insights. Remember, the most challenging times and people are our best teachers.

I know we are all busy running around from one thing to another, with too many pressures, and sometimes we feel guilty about allowing time for

---

[3] Mindful Nation UK: Report by the Mindfulness All-Party Parliamentary Group.
http://www.themindfulnessinitiative.org.uk/images/reports/Mindfulness-APPG-Report_Mindful-Nation-UK_Oct2015.pdf

ourselves. However, we can only make others happy if we are ourselves happy—it starts from inside out so just take a few minutes for yourself.

This is actually an appropriate time to cover guilt. When I was in my late twenties and went to my first coaching and therapy sessions, I felt guilty. I felt it was self-indulgent and selfish to spend money and time on this help. I even discussed it with my therapist in between the massive silences in our sessions, when I was coming to terms with actually being in therapy. I had seen my parents struggle financially and this just felt wrong. Totally wrong. However, it was the best investment I have ever made in myself.

I would not be the person I am today had I not explored the past, come to terms with it, and realigned my negative thought patterns. This guilt we experience is often about our own self-worth and esteem. Both of those are areas that will need working on, for you to have the success you want in life. If you are happy, you can make others around you happy. You can be a better mum, sister, auntie, employee, boss… you name it.

So, it's not selfish—we have to work on our inside world to improve our outside world. Give yourself time and permission. Tell yourself that you, and the people you love and respect, deserve the best you that you can be. Please don't deny yourself or others of this opportunity. Don't play small, step up. You are worth it!

PIVOTING AND SEGMENTING

There is a practice somewhat related to mindfulness. And like mindfulness, it's a tool to help you live life moment-by-moment, especially when stressful situations start to really escalate.

Take your day in segments. By this I mean consider that getting ready for work is a segment, taking the kids to school is a segment, travelling to your job is another segment... you get the idea. Briefly picture and feel how you want each day to go, piece-by-piece.

When, or if, a segment is becoming stressful, 'pivot' it... stop for a few seconds, and pause. Use your mindfulness techniques. Think about how you want to the rest of your day to go. What is next segment of your day? Getting ready to leave the house? Travelling to work? How do you want that to go?

Pivot from your current state of overwhelm and stress into a state that better suits you or you want to achieve. Take a few moments to picture it, take a deep breath and absorb it. Segmenting and pivoting doesn't mean everything will go our way, as we cannot control others, but you are better equipped to deal with people and situations. The more you do this process— stop, think about the next part of your day, pivot your mindset—the more you will enjoy your life, and not be hostage to external circumstances beyond your control. Every time you do this, the easier it gets until it's a reflex action. I do it all the time, just take that deep breath, have a 'hang on a minute' moment, and ask, "am I reacting here?" before thinking about how I want the rest of my day to go.

As a side note, planning for the future is great. However, try not to let that distract you from your day-to-day enjoyment of life. Remember; when we are enjoying ourselves and it shows, it attracts others who are in the same place, and allows for new experiences.

This all links to authenticity because you become less of a victim barrelling around reacting to situations and being taken hostage by others. You'll get to know what makes you tick, what comes up for you in these moments and what calms you and makes you happy. Keep a note of these insights.

Getting back to your authenticity

Hopefully you are now, or will be, becoming aware of:

- When you feel at risk and vulnerable, what information this gives you, and how to deal with it
- What authenticity is, why it's important, and how to give yourself space and time to figure out who you are, and what makes you tick

Let's discuss how you can become more authentic, now that you are more aware of what's going on internally. We'll use that to empower and transform your life!

Be your own detective

Whenever you feel uncomfortable, that you are not quite being yourself and trotting out something someone wants to hear... make a note, listen to it. It's your own internal BS Detector! Remember what I said before about playing with this? This is exciting and fun, as you are finding out what some people never find out about themselves. They sit around moaning about how everything else is not their fault, and that nothing can change or be changed. Have you met people like that? Are they fun, happy people to be around? No!

Do you want to have lifetime membership of the 'moan-zone' too? No... so just keep your composure, don't engage with the nay-sayers, and listen to what you are finding out about yourself? Enjoy it!

Get rid of the stuff you think you ought to say and be... authenticity means putting down the mask, leaving out the actions that don't serve you. When you find yourself just saying or doing things for the sake of it, keep a note so you can start to adapt.

One thing I want to mention here... whilst this section is about authenticity, for me at least—I don't know about you—this isn't about saying, "yeah well I'm just myself and I don't care how I come across and what people think of me." With that attitude, you may feel authentic, but it won't help you build relationships.

If that really is how you feel, go for it. However, I would like to suggest that life is fun. We are meant, and allowed, to enjoy it and save our challenges and struggles for the major things in life that we may face. Personally, I can't control what others think of me but that doesn't mean I won't put my best foot forward. It doesn't mean I don't care or give a damn about what people think about me or the relationships I have. If you want to lead a happy life with fulfilled relationships, you have to care for and nurture those connections. Even if you mess up, learn from it. I still do!

Relating to others

So much of being authentic is about connecting with others. Finding genuine connections with people you like is vital to living an authentic life. And yes, sometimes we have to relate to people we don't like or want to like, whether at work or at a family event. There may be a little facet of that person you can find a shared interest or opinion with. As much as you can though, hang out with people on your wavelength. Be interested in people. Make time for them. Listen. Ask questions. Stay in the present moment. Really engage and listen and put aside what you want to say next for now.

Forget perfect

Give yourself permission to do the best you can. It's hard when you're feeling tired and stressed but use the tools we've already discussed and allow yourself to be vulnerable in your quest for authenticity. If you want to be authentic, you'll know that you can't always be perfect, so why put that pressure on yourself? It's another way of putting on the mask and pretending things are okay when they're not.

Furthermore, accept your flaws, accept your mistakes, take ownership of them and don't beat yourself up!

Next stop, invincible and beyond...

INVINCIBILITY

TURBO CHARGE YOUR SELF-BELIEF

Invincible: "too powerful to be defeated or overcome."[4]

Why would you want to be invincible? It means you'd be unstoppable, determined, resilient, persistent. Triumphing in the face of adversity. And if you are 'game on' for living your best possible life, and going for what you want, developing a winning, invincible mindset is key. To be invincible you have to be authentic and allow yourself to be vulnerable.

But let's dig deeper, what does invincibility mean here? These are the characteristics of invincibility that have helped me personally push through:

The ability to:

- Rise above your own self-doubts and believe

---

[4] https://en.oxforddictionaries.com/definition/invincible

- Clearly identify your goals, breaking them down into bite-sized chunks and aiming for them, month-by-month, week-by-week
- Live life on your terms whilst respecting and accepting others
- Be authentically true to yourself
- Have the courage to be vulnerable
- Challenge the norm and accepted 'truths'
- Be open to change and have a thirst for knowledge
- Overcome challenges and reflect on those with gratitude
- Find and maintain balance and harmony in your life
- Stay in tune with yourself and not self-sabotage
- Have a predominantly positive mindset
- Be resilient in the face of adversity
- Be persistent in reaching your goals

It doesn't mean we are superheroes, far from it! We are all perfect, or imperfect, however you choose to see it, but accepting these basic concepts will set you well on the way to living a happy and fulfilling life.

How will adopting an invincible mindset help me?

What have you got to lose? What feels better? What do you think will get you the results you need? A glass half-empty, or a glass half-full approach? All I know is that my life seems to go a whole lot better when I adopt a positive mindset and glass half-full approach. I don't mean running away from issues, by pretending they don't exist, but facing them head on, learning, trying something new and having the faith that 'this too shall pass'. Behind most challenges there is a question that needs to be answered, so adopt a curious mindset. Think you're invincible so these issues don't drag you down. After all, who likes being around someone who is constantly negative? It's draining and I'm sure there are people you can think of, your mind screaming 'avoid, avoid, avoid.'

Exercise: find your invincible self

- What is your invincibility motto? For example, I have a few mottos or sayings that go through my mind when the going gets tough
    - Have you got your own personal slogan?
    - Or concepts of invincibility?
- When have you managed to overcome a difficult situation and turned it into a positive situation?
- Looking back, what strengths did you gain, or what lessons did you learn from that seemingly impossible situation?
- How has this learning helped you?

Invincible role models

Some of my clients have found it helpful to have 'role models' to bring to mind when needing to drum up invincible feelings, or confidence. This may be someone famous, or someone you have worked with. Mine is the popstar Pink. I like what she has to say about women, for women and her fierce, individual style. I also like that she often uses a trapeze and performs acrobatics at her concerts to ensure that her fans get the best experience and can see her up close. Talk about going the extra mile! Your role model should conjure up positive feelings and the best role models are those people who have had to fight their own battles and work hard to get to where they are. Even so-called overnight successes have put the work in.

CONFIDENCE: THE FUEL OF INVINCIBILITY

I coach a lot of people on confidence. It's a reoccurring theme. Core confidence for me is not about what you have, and you don't have. It's not the trappings of life, but a core skill set that can be learnt and it's so important to master this. With practise you can become more confidence on who are you, and the tools and exercises provided so far will help you clarify who you really are, and how to face difficult situations.

You may be confident in one situation but not in another—for example the more I practised deep sea diving, the more confident I got at it. Not complacent, but confident through drills and practise.

I enjoy public speaking, others don't. I am less confident in analysing numbers, but I can do it, it just takes me a bit longer. As you can see, we all have areas we are naturally more confident in than others. Don't write yourself off thinking 'I'm no good at it...' that's a bit of an excuse, and all the more reason to try.

When you are confident, you will not compare yourself to other people, you will accept yourself for you. This is such a huge subject, that it cannot be covered in any one book. I urge you to read further on this or get some support if you feel it's holding you back. You will be proud of your achievements, enjoy what you have done, and look to world outside rather than worry about what is going on in your head. And remember that those people who appear confident may not be—it could be a front, and even if they are genuinely confident, they'll have worked at it. Even the most successful people have times when they do not feel confident and need exercises to get them to that confident space—some people are happier in big groups of strangers, for example, but may not be so good/confident in smaller groups.

Just think how great it is to meet someone who is confident, how they make you feel around them, how they speak and hold themselves. Steal a little of what they've got and make it your own. Look at their body language, eye contact... everything. Is there someone you can think of now to emulate? Can you start to act 'as if' you have that confidence i.e. fake it or pretend? Can you close your eyes and picture your role model, or even better yourself—how you will look, be, feel and act when you are your confident self? Can you close your eyes and breathe into that state and see yourself in the starring role of that particular movie in your head?

I encourage you to try—please don't make excuses or justify staying stuck. If you want to achieve your dreams and goals, think BIG, think CONFIDENT.

Confidence will grow when you work through your vulnerabilities, when you realise who you are authentically. It will take time but don't give up!

Exercise: Confidence analysis

Try writing down or thinking about answers to the following:

- Where do I feel most confident?
- Where do I feel less confident?
- What skills and knowledge do I need to gain?
- What steps do I need to take?

Read through your answers—are they true, or excuses? What's really holding you back? You may find it's something unexpected—perhaps a belief you have about yourself, or something you are telling yourself (e.g. I'm no good at this.) that needs rewiring!

What is your self-image? Write it down and decide, is it true? What can you take action on and improve upon? Sometimes we get stuck or even hooked on feeling negative and unconfident. Or insecure.

But sometimes these old patterns just do not work anymore, and we need to get rid of them like an ill-fitting suit.

Just stay in the present and muster all the confidence you can handle.

Dealing with setbacks

Learning to live with setbacks and uncertainty, and coming out the other side, is amazing for your confidence. I had a health concern a couple of years back and I had to take it in. I thought 'well, if I believe in what I say I believe in, there really is nothing to worry about'. It was a scary time but empowering to deal with this uncertainty with confidence.

Another example... I had something happen a few years back that really floored me. Everything was going well business-wise, I was going great guns and took on a new accountant. I did the due diligence, I went on recommendation and yet they left me with a massive hole in my accounts which I had to plug. They were terrible at sorting it out and it was a significant amount. I nearly fell off my chair when I heard about it. But, thanks to having been through other major challenges in my life and learning that setbacks can be overcome, I used the 'pivoting and segmenting' technique I referred to earlier to work out what to do next. I sat down and thought 'okay, what can I do about this?' Allowing myself to be vulnerable, I asked other people and found there were more options than I had first considered. I dug deep and managed to get the issue sorted in a matter of months. I changed accountant and insisted on tighter reporting.

I questioned 'why did this happen?' What is the lesson I needed to learn? I'm not sure I figured out the why... more the fact that it happened, and I either could have sunk or swum. Sure, it put me back well over six months on my goals but maybe I needed that time to relax and regroup. The upshot is I have become much more aware of certain elements of accounting, found an accountant who works with businesses like mine, communicates with me, and gets it!!

Take the 'glass half full' (or why not 'entirely full') approach. You will overcome challenges with determination, you will learn new lessons, you will challenge the status quo, and you will find your relationships and experiences improve. What have you got to lose?

If something happens, acknowledge that it's happening. Allow yourself some quiet time to reflect, think, relax, but allow the situation to sink in.

- Be kind to yourself. Try and eat properly, sleep well, and avoid alcohol.
- Find a way to deal with those feelings. This could include crying, screaming, shouting, going for a run, going out with friends, talking to someone about the situation, watching funny films... whatever works for you and will not harm you or others.
- Speak to an expert if you need help. An independent party such as a coach, counsellor, or mentor will see things from a totally neutral position and help you work through any negative feelings you may have.

One of my favourite quotes is by Abraham Lincoln:

> *'People are just as happy as they make up their minds to be.'*

And he's right. It is a choice. There will be challenges, but these can build you not break you. Becoming invincible and happy is a choice and you can make that choice now.

Exercise: The movie of your life

Here's another exercise that my help you to cultivate an invincible mindset... think of your life as a movie poster. What poster would it be? What would the words be? Think of your life say two or five years down the track. Close your eyes, find somewhere quiet, relax and sit and connect with:

- What you are doing?
- Where you are?
- What sound you are hearing?
- Who you are with?
- How do you feel?

Really take some time to visualise this. If you want to, you can also approach this as if you are directing the movie of your life. Again, close your eyes and ask the following questions. what's happening in the movie? What is the title? What type of film is it?

You may need or want to try this a few times to what comes up. Remember this is about you and you alone—don't judge it, or block it—allow it in. This is your private work and no-one else's.

Take the information that comes to hand and write it down somewhere. Write it in a positive way in a couple of paragraphs, it's the big picture of your life. Have it displayed with pictures around it if you want. This is what I do, and I have it on display in my office to remind me why am I doing what am I doing. This may be tweaked and evolve over time—other elements may become important—and life constantly changes. But even if you are more of a detailed person, really identifying with the overall picture and owning it, will help you to start to set goals.

Really get into doing this—remember this is allowed to be fun, you are the director of your movie after all! Connect with this often to start with, the more you can sit with it, visualise and step into the picture, the more that it will seep into your subconscious and conscious mind. Set a timeframe for your picture that works for you... it may be one year, five years, or six months away.

Writing the script

You can write out the storyline as well. Getting things out of your head onto paper is priceless, it stops things swirling around in your mind. Seeing things in front of you on paper also helps you to see things objectively. To get the most out of it, write it out in the third person e.g. Sarah is doing *X* and as she does *Y*, *Z* happens. Again, have fun. Play out the story of how you want your life to unfold so you can really own it, and step into it. I've done this many times, especially when faced with a challenging situation.

SETTING GOALS

Yup, there it is. The 'G' word!! Once you've got the big picture in place, break down what you want to achieve: your goals. I am not sure you can be invincible, and achieve what you want, without knowing where you are going. Otherwise you could be wasting time and energy on what other people want, and on activities that aren't really what makes you tick.

Take a look at the areas of your life for example:

- Work and career
- Health
- Friends
- Hobbies
- Wealth
- Relationships
- Spirituality/religion
- Hobbies
- Social contribution

Most people I have worked with tend to land on eight key areas. If creative expression is important to you, add that in. On a scale of one to ten, mark down how happy are you with each area, with one being low and ten being high, and be honest with yourself. You will start to get a picture of your life in overall terms. How does that compare to your visual image, your movie? Where do you want to start?

For the areas of your life that you want to tackle, write out your goal for this area, for the year... it needs to be positive, forward looking, motivating, personal to you (no one else), and something that you can drive forward. If there are goals you seem to never progress on, ask yourself why... is it lack of time management, too much else on? How motivated are you?

Now, break down your goal into what you will do month-by-month.

The reason for breaking down the picture piece-by-piece is that if it's too big it can feel overwhelming. So, write down your goals for the year, have them in view and review them regularly. Perhaps review them each week, each day even... work out what you have achieved, what you have learnt. And ask yourself what you can celebrate... don't forget to enjoy this!

Clients often ask me how long they should spend on their goals, and my answer is that it depends on your time, money and other resources—it's whatever works for you. I think goals can have the reverse effect if you feel they are too big, too overwhelming and stopping you doing the stuff you enjoy, as you may start to feel resentful.

My advice is to enjoy them, and if the word 'goals' doesn't work for you, create your own word. I use 'venture' and 'adventures' for example, and wealth instead of finance. It works for me and gives me clarity on what I want to achieve.

However, you do it, have clear view of your own movie, your big picture, and how you will get there. As much as you can, as much as you are able, take steps every day with your goals to move yourself forwards.

Even if your goal is to kick back and enjoy life—which is a great goal—as long as you are aware of how you want to achieve that, go for it. Review your goals, enjoy the process!

A bit about balance

Depending on what values you decided on earlier in this book, what you want from your big picture, and which goals you set... balance is key. We've all heard the story of the guy that worked really hard to build their business, and their wife left them for the golf instructor, as they weren't present. Maintain that balance.

Be aware that the people in your life are important. We are human beings, not human doings, so whilst I personally have goals I want to pursue, I include ones about my relationships, as connecting with others on a meaningful level is both healthy and important. Remember to bring others on your journey with you—they may be able to help you and support you—no-one works, or enjoys life, in isolation!

Life isn't always about getting more stuff done either—there's always going to be more to do, more to achieve, so whatever you are striving for please ensure there's not a major cost elsewhere. And whatever else you do, ensure you give yourself down time.

LISTENING TO YOUR INNER CRITIC

We talked about inner beliefs and how we use that as information to propel us forward, earlier in this book, by using affirmations and positive statements, but I want to give you some additional tools here, as this may come up during your quest to be invincible.

Phrases such as 'you can't do that,' 'what did you do that for,' or 'you're so...' come from your inner critic. This inner critic comes from deep within us and if we are not careful and learn how to manage it, overcome it, and deal with it, it can paralyse us and stop us from achieving what we want in life.

That part of us is there to defend us, and clashes with the part of our mind that wants us to do well. In extreme circumstances, it can have very destructive consequences, and lead us to continue to make poor choices and stay stuck in a rut. If you feed this negative inner critic, it becomes the overwhelming voice in your mind. The inner critic also tends to zoom in on parts of ourselves we do not like, so it gives us a big clue about areas we may need to work on and develop.

There's good news though... we can overcome this inner critic by choosing to 'feed' a more positive voice within us. By becoming more aware of what our minds are telling us, we can choose a more positive voice to listen to.

How to deal with the inner critic

There are some questions to ask yourself when you hear something negative floating around in your mind. Bear in mind that we all sometimes have these thoughts, it's only human after all. You may not eradicate them overnight, but you can certainly learn how to nip them in the bud or manage them.

Accept the thought is there

Try not to push it away but play with it, question it. Maybe lighten things up. Try and relax and make notes if it will help you. I sometimes say to myself 'Uh oh… okay…' Or 'Whatever…' or 'Says Who…?' And then I ask myself some deep questions:

- What is this telling me?
- When does this voice tend to appear?
- What proof do I have this is true? How do I know this is true?
- What would my role model/friend say to me?
- How can I flip this statement into something productive?
- What would I rather think instead?

If it is a really deep, hurtful feeling you get when you hear the criticism, it is worth exploring. Try saying the statement in the third person, for example, "Jo can never get it together!" Write it out and explore how you feel about it. What reactions and feelings are coming up for you? How can you reframe this and be kinder to yourself? What can you do to be kinder to yourself? What advice would you give a friend saying this? Write it down.

You can also say, "This is not helping me. Please do not say these things as it prevents me from achieving what I want to achieve. What I really need to think is X and what I really want to do is Y. These feelings and thoughts do not serve me anymore." Write it down if you need to.

SELF-SABOTAGE

How often do we read a paper, magazine or online article, or look at a celebrity and think, 'why have they done that, when have everything going for them?" Think of Tiger Woods, Bill Clinton and many others who have reached the pinnacle of success, only to seemingly destroy it.

It's not just the rich and famous; we are all capable of sabotaging our own success. At this point, I want to recommend a book by Gay Hendricks called, 'The Big Leap' which talks about 'upper limit thinking.' In it, he explains that many of us achieve our goals, or great things, and subconsciously think, 'I don't deserve this…' and go about getting in the way of even more success or destroying what we have.

Basically, we are all capable of standing in the way of our own success. It is something to become aware of, because as you set about plans and goals for life, this notion of sabotage can creep up in the most insidious of ways!

What does sabotage look like?

Here are some examples:
- The yo-yo dieter who loses a lot of weight only to regain it
- The businessman/woman who works all hours yet struggles with personal relationships
- The person who has a seemingly happy marriage but indulges in extra-marital affairs
- The person who abuses substances, harming themselves
- The person who lurches from one financial disaster to another

Why do we sabotage?

There is a huge conflict at play here. We want something really badly, yet there is an invisible voice that rears up as we start to become successful in our quest and that doesn't want this. Maybe that side of you is comfortable with the status quo and is scared of change. Maybe that part of you will worry about whether friends or family will still be around when they see a new, improved you. It's basically a fear of change.

Here are some other examples of sabotage:

- Not doing anything—so many ideas, but the inability to follow one of them through
- Excuses... *I don't have time, money, resources*
- Quitting when it all becomes too much like hard work
- You are great at planning but less successful at finishing things
- You spend your time with people who don't add to your goals
- You don't look after yourself, so you are drained—sleep, food and nutrition, exercise
- You tell yourself you are not good enough and you don't deserve it
- You will do anything to avoid the fear of failure—or success!

How to identify your patterns

Ask yourself the following questions:

- What do I tend to do when the going gets tough?
- Where do I spend lots of time and energy that distracts from my life goals?
- What are my biggest fears about succeeding?

- What do I believe about myself?
- How realistic and true is this?
- What is a better, more positive belief I could take? Or perspective?

Tips to end sabotage

- Make goals and plans. Break down your goals into small steps and put timelines against them. Write them down and review regularly.
- Take mini-risks—try something new—take just a small step into the unknown rather than a big leap.
- Review your time. Look at how many hours there are in the week (clue: the week has 24x7 hours and that's it) and write down exactly what you spend on eating, sleeping, shopping, washing etc... and take a good look at where you can better use your time.
- Talk to yourself kindly. When you hear the negative voice, have a counter voice that says, 'it's okay I will find a way forward' or start to write down positive statements or affirmations, or say them out loud.
- Learn from mistakes. Many innovations started with failures. Many inventors, and business people had many attempts before they were successful.
- Enjoy the adventure and enjoy not knowing.
- Connect with mentors and experts., LinkedIn is great for this, for example. Find groups, mentors,

networking associations and consultants to help you and guide you.

• Reflect back. Use a journal to note down what you are learning and to note your successes along the way.

GETTING BACK TO INVINCIBLE!

Some people just seem to be brave, just as some people are born creative. However, these are actually skills we can develop in ourselves. Having courage is part of being invincible and is very important if you want to set about living life on your terms and make your dreams into reality.

Because it often means doing and being something different from what others expect or than is the norm it can be difficult, particularly at first. We all have moments of doubt and worry, that's a part of life, but allow yourself to face those times and build a courageous mindset.

To make changes to your life's direction, by definition, something or someone i.e. you, will need to change. Sometimes, it takes a while to evolve into the next phase of your life, or to shed the identity you have had to date, in order to do something different.

Sometimes we have no choice, but to be courageous—the sink or swim mentality—if you have had to deal with a big, life changing situation, or have come from a disempowering environment, congratulate yourself on wanting to grow and develop even further. Here are some tips on courage and invincibility to keep you going:

- Keep on top of your successes
- Reflect on and keep a track of your successes to inspire and motivate you when you're not 'feeling it'
- Be around courageous people
- Read books about those that have been, and are, courageous, read quotes, put quotes on your wall, or find people who you deem to be successful and courageous and spend time around them to see how they act, and deal with certain situations
- Try something completely out of your comfort zone... this will build your self -confidence and make sure you celebrate your success. It could be scuba diving, getting up on stage... just step out of what you normally do
- Learn from your past

And remember that setbacks are inevitable, everyone has them and it's what we learn, and how we adapt, that's important. Sometimes you will feel disempowered, don't bat that away, accept it for a while but don't dwell there... use these setbacks as badges of honour, like a soldier!

Nay-sayers and gratitude

One observation I would like to make is that often when we start to evolve and make changes, people do notice this change in us. So much of what I have written about in this book is increasing your own self-awareness and when you do that—especially if you start keeping a track of your progress and getting things down on paper to really process—you will feel or notice some shifts in you. You may not react in the same way to a situation that you would have previously.

You may choose not to engage in moaning, criticising or gossip, for example. It's very easy to get lifetime membership in the moan zone but it's negative energy and doesn't feed the invincible mindset at all. It detracts.

I try not to judge others, as you never know what struggles are going on with people in their own lives, but I've dealt with my fair share of extremely challenging and difficult situations. They were tough, but I was invincible from a young age because I had to be it was about survival, 'sink or swim.'

I want invincible to be more than survival for you: living a life less normal and more extraordinary, because the normal can be to complain about your lot and makes you unhappy.

I've actually had people walk up to me and say, 'How come you're so happy?' I just smile because I have spent many, many years practising and using the tools I discuss in this book and more. And know how to live invincibly.

There's so much more I could write on the energy you put out to other people, but that's a different book. Suffice to say when people ask 'where do you get your energy from' that I have my very clear answer. I follow my own advice!

What I am saying is 'don't let the buggers drag you down' and trust me when I say I am writing this with a smile on my face. There is so much I am grateful for, and if you think about, there's so much you can be grateful for. Try and think of five things every day and write them down. The more you do it, the more things you will find, and realise you can be grateful about. It's like exercising a muscle, the more you do it, the easier it gets… and so much of this book is about exercising different mental muscles!

I sometimes visualise myself in bubble wrap, or with a white light around me, if I feel moaners are invading my space. What is remarkable though, is that the more I have adopted this mindset and used the other exercises, the less I tend to be around those kinds of people anymore. Or at the very least I limit my time with them.

MEDITATION

I can't write this chapter without referring to meditation. Practising this on a regular basis gives you such insights into your thoughts, and gives you space to think about those thoughts. It also slows down your reactions, so you are more in charge of your experiences; it's relaxing, increasing the oxygen flow in your body and there is sufficient clinical evidence around meditation[5] for it to be recommended by many health professionals today. It has been found to:

- Increase immunity
- Increase emotional balance
- Reduce blood pressure, pain and other health concerns
- Improves quality of life
- Release stress and anxiety
- Improve attention span
- Improve quality of life

There are CDs, soundtracks, and plenty of videos on YouTube to help you find the right meditation method for you. Sometimes, I like listening to affirmations or binaural beats as a type of meditation, other times I prefer silence to allow my thought to flow; I don't hang on to them, I let them go. Even if it's a few minutes each

---

[5] https://nccih.nih.gov/health/providers/digest/meditation

day, meditation allows me to stop, pause, and relax, so find yourself a quiet space. I sit in my back garden or in a chair with the back door open and breathe in fresh air whilst sitting there with my eyes closed.

There are also many mediation groups you can join, if you'd rather find people to explore it with, and these are invaluable to get you started and meeting like-minded people. Or you can also meditate by walking. Find a place where you can breathe deeply and get into your zone.

Even if you are in a stressful situation, the ability to stop, close your eyes for a few seconds and take a deep breath, allows you to gather yourself and your thoughts, so you don't react in a lower self-way. It gives you the time and space to be fully present and fully you.

I would start with a few minutes each day and build up from there. If you have never done meditated before, sitting in quiet space, doing nothing whilst used to being in a noisy world may feel odd, but you will get used to it.

I miss it now if I don't do it, and if you want to become invincible, meditation is key to reconnecting with yourself, and learning to stop, pause, and just let go!

BRINGING IT ALL TOGETHER

We've taken quite a journey from vulnerability, through to being invincible, via learning to be authentic.

It's been a whistle-stop tour of the different elements of this three-part process. Along the way, I've explained how it's helped me personally, why it's important, and provided some exercises for you.

I use these techniques and tools myself and have studied and read as much as I can, to become the best version of myself I can be. This is how it's helped me and my clients:

- Make sense of difficult situations and triumph from them
- Improved relationships
- Better career prospects and planning
- Better business results
- High performing colleagues and teams
- Identification and achievement of goals
- Overcoming and pivoting from challenging situations and people
- Increased strength, vitality and well being
- Better time management
- Less overwhelm
- Increased happiness and unstoppable energy

I've managed to leave successful careers to start new ventures when everyone was telling me not to, left relationships and found a great person to accompany me on my journey, increased my wealth, helped countless other people, dealt with health issues face on, taken up new hobbies, even those that were really challenging such as running half marathons.

And overall, I'm much happier. I feel on course. Life is not always the proverbial bed of roses—we may get scratches, but they can heal as long as we decide we are going to be INVINCIBLE!

Use this book as your guide. Start keeping a journal of your progress and get in touch with me to explore some of these issues in more detail, and to find out how they can help you or your organisation. You may also find the following free resources helpful:

https://sarah-j.com/free-coaching-resources/

ABOUT SARAH JONES

Sarah Jones is a seasoned personal, life, business and career coach. Born with an entrepreneurial spirit and an insatiable drive to help others find their happiness, she founded her successful coaching business to help people find purpose, meaning and direction in their lives and careers. Sarah has been through many of the roadblocks and challenges she coaches on, herself so is able to empower others to identify and reach their full potential.

As a qualified coach in personal, corporate and executive coaching, Sarah runs Sarah-J Coaching. She provides products and services that help people and businesses bust through blocks, identify a clear path and navigate their lives, careers, and businesses to fulfil their individual ideals of success.

She works with individuals on a one-to-one basis for personal and career coaching; and both on a one-to-one and group basis for businesses. She has also devised several programmes to help people personally to reach their desired potential. Sarah is also a regular speaker and media commentator.

She is based in Hertfordshire, UK and has local, national and international clients.

To find out more about Sarah's coaching programmes for individuals, executives, teams or organisations visit:

https://www.sarah-j.com

SUCCESS STORIES

"Sarah helped me to raise awareness about my strengths and consider new possibilities..."

The sessions with Sarah have had an extremely positive impact in my life and important kick-start moving toward setting up my business. Setting up a new business is, at the same time, very exciting and overwhelming. With Sarah, I was able to have a clear idea of how I could to move forward, with an action plan. Sarah's invaluable experience and coaching techniques help me to raise awareness about my strengths and considering new possibilities that increased my motivation to work towards my goal. I would like to take this opportunity to thank Sarah for her time, patience and support turning my dream into my reality. I highly recommend Sarah to anyone looking into setting up a new business, as I believe Sarah is a GREAT inspirational coach. Thank you.

"Delivered results beyond my expectations."

Prior to the sessions with Sarah I think I've been too distracted and concerned by my weaknesses; I often took my weaknesses out of context hindering my career progression. I now have some 'tools for life' in particular I constantly reframe situations/issues and this has been fundamental to me in developing a more positive approach to dealing with challenges; some of which I may have avoided all together in the past. It is with great pleasure I'm able to say I have tried and tested the approaches I have developed from these sessions. They have delivered results beyond my expectations but more importantly to me, I have delivered these results without being stressed to the hilt and not feeling like I'm sprinting on a treadmill just to keep things on an even keel. Instead, I'm motivated and at a fulfilled level whilst also delivering some great results. Thanks for everything Sarah; it was a pleasure and life changing."

For more success stories, visit:

https://sarah-j.com/success-stories/